COOL, CRUEL WORLD

By Iona May Todd

If You're Reading This, You're The Diary Page I Didn't Rip Up:

Dear Diary,

I won't make this poetical, and lyrical, like I try so hard with the rest of my words – I do that because the words don't trickle out of me so well when I talk, and it pains me to think of how I sound to another, but that is not important. What is important, is that I am scared of fate. I am not scared in the slightest of much, but adrenaline is like heroin to me, anything could happen to me but I still don't seem to care. What it is that I seem to be scared of, is the fact of the life that I belong only to the inside of my little, indistinct mind of mine. There I am.

I am stowed inside of hitchhiked cars, making my way from motel to hotel to motel when I probably have no money in my pocket, peering under steaming petrol station night lights, dancing in the purest form of the dark, sitting between the coloured dirt in a normalized suburbia.

First of all, it seems Americanized ideas have penetrated my thinking, and there is no way of getting there when I am only a waitress with a cherry sweet smile which some of the men say capture them. I have an archaic tongue, but that won't get me far, not in this cruel world I've come to know. This is the first fear – of how I make it to the place I seem to yearn.

There are no motels here, and no sense of fortitude of aspirations to do something more than what the people say the day already dictates, which I have seen on anybody's face who passes me when I walk to nowhere in particular. Then again, I suppose my face will neither tell of sweet nothings of freedom, and of dreamy ambitions that seem so credible in my conjuring's. Then I think again, and you cannot know a person, cannot command their own way of wants. You must go it alone.

I have always gone it alone, this far.

During the night, one day, I sat alone at midnight, under the light – snuck out to see what would happen and who would pass me by, so this time I could try and find someone to talk too, just to say hi. Incidentally on that occasion, the world but me was asleep.

One afternoon, I ran with barely any clothes on, the rain beating against my plump skin, from my house to the forest, and sat to be drenched and ask the world every nihilistic cry I had in me. I called a friend, told her I how much I wondered how it would feel to die. She hung up.

The night seems to breed me, as you can see, and another time, I drank in my room and danced for hours in the dark, and not even a single person went by my window. Somehow whenever I gauge life, everybody else disappears. And where do they go? It would have been nice to know, but now it seems not so important when I think about it.

I aforementioned a 'first of all,' which to those of structure, would be the primary to the secondary of 'secondly.' And you're right.

But I do not have a second of all, or any other infinitesimal 'at all's,' at all. I wish I did. I wish I could stand to sift through my thoughts of flour but for all of the tearful ideas and words which flit in my mind throughout my times, I cannot recall a single one. It's all there, and I'd show you if I could, to help you really see what I meant, if you wanted.

Then again, maybe I'd filter it first, because it is healthy to keep secrets, and of all, I am best at that. All this time, I have been able to smile and shush, I don't know if out of choice, just out of what became.

I was always there, through life – was there, when was I really at all? You'd have to ask.

I'd like to go on but I am distracted, so I will find a way to finish this passage of time even when I never really finished the days I'd articulate on paper as a wayward youth, but here you go. For you.

For the paper of the wood with sharp sawdust and eyes of blue. For you, for I seem to be more of you, than I am of what I should be.

A Woman Is A Tree

There is
a girl.
An indeterminate confusion, yet a forever delusion,
where her hair knots into the bark of her skin.
Eyes two blossoms of tulips
mouth ground ripe with two lips,
sweet, sweet salvia tasting like venom.
She has brewed into poison oak.
You ask who matted her so.
Here, finds so much curiosity, undulating in the waves of the breath which
does not only come from her mouth,
but also from her steaming pores, and the hairless holes gaping in her legs and
arms
left from you,
as you so asked.
Blackened petals where her eyelashes blink
so her eyes do sink
and her mind does drink
the music breezes through her lungs.
Cemented, her feet no longer dance, nor do her fingers to the beat of men,
when instead they are choked, by roots which say they are the Earth,
whilst the only question posed
is how an *Earth* so beautiful, can spew branches so horrific, prolific
magnificently soporific.
Still,
she finds her ways.
The ways her mother birthed into her and cannot be so easily snipped as her
fingernails or her skin,
to peel away the flowers from her stomach lining
And to sprout them out through her fingertips.
The curve, or the meridian of her hips,
Engrained into your body like the sand of the beach,
naked but dowsed, in teardrops of heaven
yet which leave her stitched to the same ground she has been all this time.
You say you can't find her but have looked
rooted in lies, when she has been here all this time.

Time is grown from her dress of ivy, and her hands of soil
waiting beyond a heart of trodden blades
of grass
with toes of leaves, eyes of green
holes left in the world.
And for all this simplicity
of what it means to see
her rotten little soul
was so dirty that it died.
Never was set free.

Virgin Divine

Don't make it harder for me.
Make me speak.
Think you will force me then call me quiet and weak.
I walk through life with a soft gaze filtering over my eyes,
falling in love with every pretty thing
like the pink lemonade of sun on the grass and
the fertility of white light easily forgiving on our skins, sins.
I have slideshows of carnage in my mind
and I dream of bleeding
falling in love all over again
with the memory than I ever did with the reality.
All this time, I keep myself to myself
I'm one of the girls,
synching my lunar rhythms up to fit in.
My breathing makes me a girl
My moaning makes a woman,
Together makes a whore
So why did you call me an enigma?
Open up the files of my mind in trade for my legs
because I am not the marrying type
just have fingertips stained with blood and wine
tell me I'm perfect
call me virgin divine
because I'm selfish like that
and you can't make me
I'll shout and I'll scream but surely you're never wrong
so I wonder how long I'll last for
before I realise heavenly is the new whore.

Dahlia's In The Window

People are scared of something beautiful when it's vacant,
Like a hollow honeyed sunrise
Or doll's head without it's eyes
A pretty girl depressed – it's not worth it.
Maybe that's why I'd prefer to run,
when I pass the widowed house,
to skip the charred wood doors sprinkled in poppy-seed blemishes,
and pass on the rosy blood bricks,
the whole place diluted in the daffodil spots of sun,
because it scares me when I walk by
so much, I go quick, I can't help it I want to cry
smelling the insides that seep out of the open windows
smelling like old times and piss
I go quick, I want to cry.
I look inside, because there are no blinds
and it feels wrong, exposed,
like a naked body after losing its drawers,
what with mahogany scars and dulled colours
dead flowers on the windowsill aching, broken-backed.
I don't understand who changes them each week
when I could be sure no one lives there at all.
There are lambs ears, drooping with sadness,
or unbrushed maidenhair by the next week,
snapped head of white lilies,
beige and cream, living barely.
I could ask who changes flowers in a vacant house,
but I don't,
I just look because I can
fresh in death
going quick, because I don't want to be here longer than I am.

She

She lulls herself with rhyme
All her life she has dreamed she would shine
On the stage like a puddle of oyster brine
where reality is not real
and she doesn't have to be the Her for this one time.
She tends to visit the beach, sleeps at night and wakes with sand in her hair
that she does not wash back out.
She dreams of getting out, growing up, and going away to never come back
and has pictured herself for years on the open road.
She cannot bare to stay, and will always leave, because nowhere is her home if
everywhere in the world is begging for her body.
She'll save if she must
use money that only has matter in the present
to make it somewhere where she can truly be it
wild as an animal like the kids would call her when she was young.
She still has dreams
dreams that become more when she looks and smiles in the mirror
but where is she to start?
She stays as she would
out at night, looking the streets for ambition or experience
wanting strangers to come up to her in their fancy old car, speaking just to stay friendly
give her a ride if they might, nothing else on their minds.
Find themselves some place, that okay?
Sure.
She wakes in spring fields, daisy chains on her wrists
shedding her skin to blend in.
But what is she to do?
This always happens.
Me
and I cry every day
for the sea, the sun, the sky, and The She.

He

I don't know if I meant for this to happen
and I am sorry I cannot find my way as clearly in the day,
not a nocturnal creature but a one
of maybe just halfway;
I don't mean to rhyme, I'm just distracted by some way
but I try to breathe like I've ever been able,
and tell myself
I just dance by myself
okay.
Okay what I mean is,
what I think…
no.
To know?
I think,
I dreamt during the day
With a soft sepia light, and red cups filled with water that tasted expired,
I couldn't see straight so fell and felt it first.
Where your stage became a lightning show for my droopy eyes that were too curious to be wide
I couldn't see at all.
Blazing claustrophobia had been burning me by the bit,
because I had tasted the scent of feeling
and had seen the sound of what I thought was myself;
but was you.
That is how I felt.
There must have been a mirror in the floor and I never want it to crack
because there's too much good luck in you to turn me bad.
There.
where
your liquid eyes drank me so fluently as if you recognised my taste
a one I hoped you wouldn't just make up,
spinning me by my ends into the purest living gold
because as I loved you, I really loved you
so I cried and I died but survived because I could stand the pain.
And my life became by you;
the artist and author of what I knew,

like a god but not of the usual kind.
To become your baby but one a little more mature.
But it's not as if I mind
that I had to suffer til then to breathe like I must have before birth,
but
I can't find the words anymore
I was never good with speech at all.
Not much good for a lot,
but to see you in a way I knew no one else could,
would.
I don't know what I'm saying, yet I hear you so well,
where my toes are covered in the chocolate ground and I lie down on the mint
flavoured grass
where I can play, and can be
as you watch me like you did
as long as I am free
and I love you like I do
when it was just you
and it was just me.

You Boulevard

The sail is white. My boat was white
I never travelled during the day
the sea only ever was strongest at night.
I tell you everything but I've liked keeping this to myself
because the stars might have seen me but they promise they'd never tell –
they're just as you're your friends as well.
They didn't see me in the light
felt my figure, heard my paddles
and I went slowly and lightly
I had to be careful.
Can I believe it?
She can't believe it.
I was a figure without a dress, with a white sky and a black surface
sailing from poles north to south
in a world made from glass.
In the night I climbed the mountains,
but you know that because you counted my footsteps
upon the ground you constructed, raising mountains with those hands
that charmed all of town.
What with your wilting willows and your wiry veins
I was wrapped in rainfalls of your bleeding,
and needing,
ringing of the dark meshed with your colour, be it bloody.
I could not keep going.
I had to stop the sailing
my soul and body is flailing, and upon you is my feeding
to swallow you whole in one kiss of gasping freshness
so you have an insider's look at how it is possible for black to turn bright.
I can't keep writing
I think my wrists were broken
snapped like dry wood, my sharp muscles like spelk.
But in telling you this, it is not pain that I felt.
I hear two hearts, but I lost my sight,
cannot read. Cannot write.
You got mine, deep from under my chest
those hands again, feeling me by the inside

the fallen walls, the bubbly boiling of my blood
pulling out the poetry inside of me and spilling.
There's a cat in the yard,
beside the car, next to the kids.
We can hide
Together it keeps us alive
trailing down the hills we crafted when we were their age.
Remember that time?
Thank heavens that your mine,
All this time and you are still frighteningly fine
All this time, and we've never misaligned.
I must have been joking, because I could never have been blind,
when no one owns eyes like the ones that I do
to see you alight, a-flight, so light, a sight
that brings the senses back that I lost.
You seem to shine, and I cure as you rise
the world can feel my footsteps this time round
on our journey around the poles
and you've given me back my feelings.
Pick me apart with your flurry,
just please come with me. Hurry.
I promise we will never be found.
With my sailing partner, I've retired.
To the shore we descended,
the two bodies that created the Earth, watching it grow old.
Look,
hard, not with your eyes. Behind them.
See it?
We lost track of it.
It's blue, and we're not.
We are sucked through the decades, surviving in spots where nothing else could,
becoming what's left of the world we watched,
we began.
All this time, and we lost track of it.
So the sound has gone again, alike the senses,
but I think I prefer it that way

it means I have no sense but you,
just how I should.
It feels good,
where there's no existence but for me and for you
old and holding hands, walking down the avenue.

Mr Mob's Wife

I've waited for you
with my curled hair wound in the getaway car door.
Torn tights
sick sights
my cuts look like zebra stripes
white go-go boots clinging to my legs
holding for dear life, dangling in the back seat.
Those men left food in my teeth and bit my tongue
I spit on the car seats and hock up my lungs
the cocktails you told me to drink on my tastebuds
that you said would make me hit the roof,
but your men know more about that than me.
I might be gone by the time you get to me,
Hurry up.
Fuck.
I'm waiting for you
Sobbing off my lashes, sick of being your girl
my sex your weapon
is that why you call me Pea? I'm Plutonium?
Give me time, I scream
as you fall in the front, fucking over the ignition
Don't look at me, before I'm ready for you
just step on it before I blow,
nuclear fission.
But I'm still waiting for you,
blood on my hands, on my lips.
My fists and face go blue, baby
banging on the window for you to get me
come save me.
I'm waiting for you, beat them before they have me
I know you'll call me a slut
but I tried to fight it all I could
even when they cut you out of me, my legs were firmly shut
but you can't make me now, baby,
don't say you did all you could.

I Did All I Could

Look at them
Holding hands because two makes one
Whole to ascend
Through the heavens to finally meet again.
He caught her on the way down
Carried her to bed
To be beside her so that she could sleep sound, hands on her waist and head.
Two beings bound by one solution
Being only for absolution, that being alone is not an option
For her, for him
For copulation
Feeling inside each other to recognise
The sign of the times they remember
Recognising the disillusion
That the soul they want to be there
Is there
When they ask who's in.
Forever wed, in heaven
Flowers that bud and you can stick in
Your hands and taste the obsession, one being
Flavours of lemon and elderflower, not too sweet
Because they are all they will ever need
They remember from last time
Walking by the tides, her gaping into his kind eyes
His kisses all over her thighs
Undictated by rhyme, and time as they age
Only what is, forever will be
Back through the skies to be alive or to die
Feels just as good
To be together.
I wish it were the case.
I did all that I could.

Groupie Girls

You don't understand the things I would do –
Fuck the world over if you wanted me too.
Your voice stays sighing
I felt in on my thighs,
That's what all the girls say,
gossiping as you shine.
We all say the same
It's not lame when the person we know you as stays different.
You tell us,
with salt in your locks and eyeliner down your cheeks,
You say,
Each one of you girls makes me feel some way. You're mine.
We're yours
in a firing line like a daisy chain
shoulder to shoulder with our knees weak and mouths open
counting the inches your hair grows, all of us staying hoping.
Your mind is wild and I love that about you.
You sing and sing like a child, and we copy – I want to be like you.
The wilderness is beautiful, nobody sees it like you do.
No one understands you like us, down on the ranch dancing the bugaloo,
your girls want as much of the world as you do
you know better than we do.
We know better than they do,
That you're divine, that's why
Not sick or mean like the papers lie
but that's why we love you
made just for you,
your groupie girls, my leader
We'd die for you, I feel it.

Suicide Blonde

I'd like for you to catch me
before I bounce off the ground
And crack into two halves of a nothing.
I'm fresh from the ocean
but I have to tell you about how I'm barely coping.
I wake up and I'm either choking
or vomiting up leftovers and moonshine
like the guys at club when you tell me I'm fine.
I could be yours
I could be rotten, full of mould spores and horrors
a baby doll whose head exploded.
I'm an angel-face dusty and eroded.
I'm a bombshell, eating myself like a cannibal.
I swallowed your jewellery
so my insides and intestines could be pawned for gold chains.
I'm black and I'm blue, I'm a mess, I didn't think this through.
He let me.
I didn't care, it's whatever.
Told me that dying now would mean I could live this way forever.
I breathed in your CO_2, poisoning myself so I can fly.
But I decide last minute that you're wrong, I don't want to go –
That is how she died.
For him, by him, but by her own
so I can't blame him, it was her
She was looped; a fucking souvenir.
He liked to play girl roulette,
glad she wasn't there to find out
that he preferred brunettes.

Finish

The way I'm high,
Charged up with battery fluid through my hands
Sometimes makes me fluid
Sometimes makes me mad
Feels like I'm wired
With an extra eye to see through these lies
that I'm telling and I'm told
Because I thought thinking was private but seems like I've poured myself out on the street,
for everyone to see.
Asks me where I went
Asks me where I go
I threw up on myself and it goes all over the floor.
Car-light, dash-light screws me so I just might
Jump and glide, tell everyone I died
Close my eyes and see it happen for myself
As if it doesn't, even when I'm open
Legs open and arms wide
I'm stuffed full with fluff and love inside
Heavy,
Might fall off the side
Falls off the side
Tell me
to
Fall off the side
Out of
the light
Treat me like I'm sick
I'm just as sick as they think
I'm stuffed with carnage and evil and zinc.
They think
They think?
I think
I think I'm –
You're sick
I'm useless

I'm useless and I'm hopeless
Now I'm sleepless
All of
the time
Sometimes
being is pointless.
Is it really?
It's really
sick to think that I could
buy into my dreams but it's not for lack of trying
When in those barren lands, I search whilst I'm nameless
And now I'm fuzzy and forever faceless
Less than I am but for when I am anxious
But I said I
wouldn't feel it
Won't feel it
Feel it, steal it
I said that I'd lose it
But I'd choose it
And I wouldn't finish.
I would excuse it.
And I wouldn't —

Join The Club

"And so he grabbed me, and he told me, Baby, I said Baby, what?, and he said Baby, I think I'm flying."

Space-like starlight of the gas station lamp light is shining like it's supposed too. I say it like it had to be there, but it's just there, and I wonder. Who turns the gas station lights on?

The clerk, with her grapefruit eyes, chewing her grape-flavoured gum, looks at me through the window, beneath a midst of midnight, out here, beneath the gas station light, finally, because I've been dancing around for the last hour just in the hopes she'd look.

Clerk sees me. Hi, Clerk.

"When I close my eyes, I think I'm flying. And I think I feel toe tips pressing against the inner skin on my stomach, things writhing around in my intestines, but I'm pretending not to notice, baby."

My truth is that I dare not speak.

I think if I use my eyes, lids, lashes and all, that I can convey something better than the blue gem in my throat can. He doesn't know how to communicate.

They never do, do they? Hahaha, tell me about it.

What do you think I can tell you that isn't already so obvious? Am I just oblivious?

What can I do to make you look at me, looking at you, and spit your fucking gum out on the floor already so I can make you fucking understand that things out here are so much more important than to stand there and watch and wait like things are coming to you you banana shaped fuck look at the real world for how it really truly is.

'It's like, I can see this woman seeing me, even with my closed eyes. But where am I? I'm – I'm, 'You're you, like I've always told you,' she says.'

I don't know where I am. I could give you an answer, but you haven't asked for one so I am not willing to waste my breath. Does that make me a hypocrite? That I'm talking right now and every thought, word, symbol is fiction that I've made up.

Like this. What is 'this'?

What's that?

Does this make a difference. What do I do with that!

How do I convince you? Do I even. Do you even. A generation that I am watching from beneath the weeping light, fleeing, feeding into the background until the molecules of their shadows pass away, because that someone, whoever that someone, eventually turns the lights off.

'Baby, I'm leaving, today. It doesn't matter anyway because I know you'll be coming with me, one way or another, when you get this all figured out.'

What figured out?

'And I look forward to figuring it out with you when you're normal again.'

Who made that up?

'And when you feel your feet on the ground again, gimme a call.'

Give you a call, pfffsssht. Give you a call with the cord wrapped in my asshole – listen to all of my shit all over again. Leave a voicemail so the clerk can too, hear loud and clear.

What's the point? Tniop eht stahw? Am I still making sense.

So, how at all, does this? Do I?

What sense have you made out of all this, and what sense have you made out of me

you banana shaped fucks?

Holly Wood

Camera lights
Starlight
Moonlight
Fame fights the bold
Favours the controlled
The name of my lip gloss is 'Cool Girl: Ice Cold.'
She steps on starry faces in the floor
Hurried like a puppy through the wailing crowd.
They call out her name like a dog
Fans looking at her like she were a god
feeling old and hazy, soft trauma under her fingernails.
She has to dance, otherwise she's useless
but don't tell her, keep her clueless
put her on stage 'til she's restless
then bring her back to my room until
she's defenceless and her friends get jealous.
Holly likes smiling, her mouth round like an apple pie,
her head itchy and burnt from the bleach,
just it's generally miserable, this living.
It always makes its way underneath.
I'm an entertainment piece, getting older 'til I'm not a girl
Leave her looks 'til last
Just break everything else first, it'll work.
By her grave there is nothing but grass
Just conspirators and manipulators, liars, murderers and thieves, or whoever died last.
Miss Wood is just like the trees,
a movie-star with arthritis sunken into her like disease
The pictures of her perfect living like she were theirs,
dead now so she can't speak, and so you can't talk about her settled despair.

Dahlia's In The Window Part 2

Lamb's ears can't hear
but they've turned dark since the other day,
dripping onto the windowsill,
flaky like dust.
They've turned as black as sin
looking out at me as I look in.
I thought she was a mannequin
her smile like silver, all femininity pulled out from within.
Dahlia's behind the window pane,
sad eyes and dark shadows like tar on her white skin.
There are dahlia's on the windowsill, itchy to be free.
Probably won't be solved
Probably never will be.
She's like an actress behind the glass, begging for water
beside flowers dying of thirst.
Dahlia's in the window
Her eyes are spoilt with soil
rooted back into the grass but couldn't regrow
by intestine by organ by organ by bowel
I can see Dahlia in the window, and never know who took her from the sill.

But I'll Keep Looking

I think I've lost my head –
Either on the stove or down the bed.
Either way, I'll leave it there,
Didn't need it today, anyway
when I walk my way past the lakes, the roads and the bay
I look for you, each step of the way
Through the cars,
In the windows
As if I am the lost soul of some old widow
Is that what I have come too?
The type of girl who leaves her pinafore askew, and asks too few questions to
at all be noticed?
Through all of the blue
Now, I've misplaced my husband, too
Surely
he's somewhere in the garden
Maybe sat, waiting for me, in the trees
I admit, there is not much that has become of me
But I thought you wouldn't mind
if my mind begins to wander whilst I walk
adrift down the street amidst the dawning world
or perhaps
Simply somewhere looking for you
wherever you've gotten too
On the stove, in the bed –
I'm sure I can find you somewhere
just got to find where I put my head.

I'm So Cool, I'm Dead

What can I do?
If the answer isn't loving you
then I don't want to hear it.
I stand here like I'm a girl who wants to dance, or who would rather be smiling
in my high heels, quietly dying with the lights flashing in my eyes.
If I could feel maybe it would be easier,
because I'd rather be high than here
than anywhere.
More of me wants to be less than, with the music pounding,
I'm waiting to be degraded, begging to be.
It's all I know
paired with my soft melancholy.
I'm not sure what I'm used to
or what the girls expect of me.
I'm what all the boys expect me to be,
less than their time and less than my breath
so if I go home,
when they all notice, I hope they don't care
and should only feel the gap of me left there.
It's warmer in here than out there.
I can smell the sourness of my kitchen tiles,
see the baking powder left on the bench
I can drag my feet in here and no one would care.
I can take my clothes off and still somehow be more than my body in here.
I don't have to pretend that I'm sad or I'm happy.
It's warmer in the bath and I take all of my pills with me.
What can I do?
I am thinking about you, really busy loving you
sometimes too lazy to do anything about it.
Pumping myself with red, blue, green and pink pills feels good
but I'm too tired to taste them going down like pieces of rubber or cardboard.
I'm awake nearly enough to choke
sadly I don't, but I keep trying.
And it feels better, forgetting about you
I think that I'm cool but maybe I'm kidding myself
convincing myself that I'd find you

be it in my words or on my mind.
The bathroom tiles are harder, and they are cold on the back of my head
but soon enough, that goes away too
replaced by the softness of the water.
It's better than I could have thought.
I thought it wouldn't be you, when the room gets slower and dreamy.
I should be the coolest,
grinning when I'm sad,
like the writer of the worst poetry,
because there you are, feeling for me.
I couldn't stop being your baby, not even if I tried.
Call me silly, tell me you're just in my mind,
Because even if you're right,
at least now I'd never have to find out.

Pink Bathroom Tiles

She was lying there
in the bathtub
the tides of her life climaxing in her eyes
thinking about where to go next, in her paused mind,
silky, dirty bathtub water dripping down her nose
and the bubbles of prosecco left foaming at her mouth
like a rabid animal
private, but it's personal.
And I didn't know what to do
but to look at the ants on the walls
free to dance now that she was too dead to glance,
ones from the ceiling
toppling, face first
in a deep dive between her thighs, into the lilac water below.
Jeronimo, Jeremy, Jerome
let it go
It's here she's so happy that she could die.
And she was lying there
in the bathtub,
pills of glitter in her blood.
Sodden and pruning, frosted eyes
that I'd eat up
cereal bowl for a head, bath milk on her legs and fingers
either focused or forgetting
just like a painting
pink bathroom tiles spanning for miles
in the death days and her DNA
XX rating.
She's dripping
down the side of the tub
hanging fingers parted, blue and cream, on the lip of it
left herself to go cold and hard, moaning, fuming at every drip.
She's lying here
in the bathtub
died a couple days ago
leaks out onto the floor

naked and dead, what is she waiting for?
Closes her eyes, she turns to ice, melts and condenses
not for attention
feels for ascension
but stays in the tub instead.

Tropico

Come get me
In my cage, chains around my neck, wrists and waist
dripping in nakedness and my gold soul
peeling from my tongue
down my legs,
bursting out my bars because I don't fit.
Limes in my eyes and I still can't see right in front of me
Because this pain is blinding, thorns dug deep into my chest
spine acupunctured, but at least my blood tastes like rose
infant zinfandel left on the side
by the fresh flowers
because of the one you've put inside.
Pineapple pain with apple sweet thoughts,
I'm tropical and you like that
I'm tropico because you stopped me when I tried
to tell you.
I'm tropic-
Oh.
I'm tro
ublemaking
and I'm
oh
raging
setting alight the flames of my nerves
You're watt?
I'm heavenly, tropically
dying to play,
He must know that I will not stay.
He must know that I smell like skin,
singing my hymns
falling to the floor and running 'til I'm away from him.
Outside, these insect bites are kisses,
grass soft blades of luxury.
The night is singing for me
and I cover myself in feathers.
Like the scars and birthmarks that I can't see

whispers feelings I should remember –
how I may love you,
or leak unbuttoned your adoration of me
but I am not yours.
I will leave, no less.
Gardens of yellow bells shush on me,
humming into my harp of hearts,
Carrying me until I'm safe, lying in a duvet of crops.
I shower myself in the rain
fresh flowers sprouting from my veins
Here I am, Lord.
It's my soul before my body,
a phantom figure of mother who belongs everywhere not
                                      here.
Morning dew clings to me like film
feeling in the pits of me to find the child who begged to live free,
who begged to be beyond the Earth
not in it.
The one who loved to love, abducted by spirit.
Birds of paradise flock to me like I were a landing spot,
chirping and talking on my tree branch wings.
They lie to you,
the dreamers.
I am an open rose cut from thorn,
listening to the lies on the breeze.
She died free.
I don't feel.
I trust no one.
Watch me when I flee.

Iona May Todd

I'm going

I'm going

I'm gone.

Don't try to find me

¿Puedes encontrarme?

I've told myself this is it

that I'm tired of making sense.

We could still be friends

but I've already told myself that I'll never write again.

Printed in Great Britain
by Amazon